Contents

W9-AIA-595

Keymap

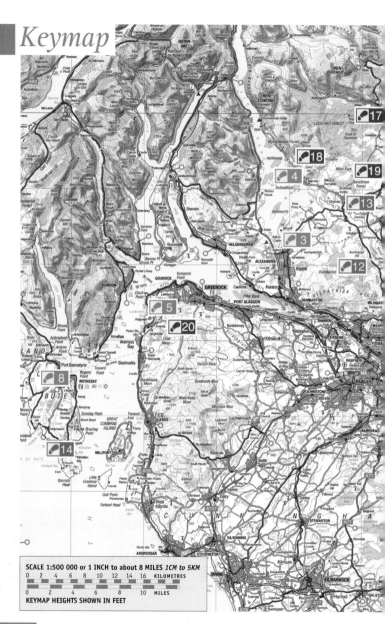

SCALE 1:500 000 or 1 INCH to about 8 MILES *1CM to 5KM*

0 2 4 6 8 10 12 14 16 KILOMETRES

0 2 4 6 8 10 MILES

KEYMAP HEIGHTS SHOWN IN FEET

Introduction

The routes and information in this book have been devised specifically with families and children in mind. All the walks include points of interest as well as a question to provide an objective.

If you, or your children, have not walked before, choose from the shorter walks for your first outings, although none of the walks is especially demanding. The purpose is not simply to get from A to B, but to enjoy an exploration, which may be just a steady stroll in the countryside, alongside rivers and lakes, through woodlands or climbing hills.

The walks are graded by length and difficulty, but few landscapes are truly flat, so even short walks may involve some ascent, although this is nowhere excessive, and even on Tinto, the highest summit in the Clyde Valley, a steady plod will suffice. Details are given under Route Features in the first information box for each route, but the precise nature of the ground underfoot will depend on recent weather conditions.

If you do set out on a walk and discover the going is harder than you expected, or the weather has deteriorated, do not be afraid to turn back. The route will always be there another day, when you are fitter or the children are more experienced or the weather is better. Few of the walks in this book involve rough terrain (although there are a number of steep grassy slopes, a couple of exposed summits and some muddy going after rain), but it is always advisable to wear proper walking footwear rather than trainers or wellington boots, and to take wind- or water-proofs.

Bear in mind that the countryside is constantly changing. Landmarks may disappear, gates may becomes stiles, rights-of-way may be altered, permissive paths may close. In quite a few places the terrain can be confusing, and this means having to pay rather close attention to route descriptions and waymarking or, in the absence of waymarking, the general direction followed by the path. But none of the walks is so complex as to deter anyone.

Highland cattle at Pollok

A few of the paths are seasonally overgrown, or may be affected with wind-damage. This presents two problems: one is difficulty in following the route underfoot; the other is the soaking you may get from overgrowth if you do the walk after rain, or stinging by nettles, which will be a problem for young children. It also makes the wearing of shorts something to be wary of.

Because many of the walks venture into remote areas of woodland, moorland or mountainside it is a good idea to get into the habit of carrying a small daysack containing waterproof clothing, spare clothing against a chill wind, something to eat and drink (preferably a warm drink, although bottled water is fine on a hot summer's day). Always take a map and compass, and the knowledge to use them safely; if you are not expert with maps, these walks generally would be a good place to develop your skills.

Around Glasgow

For many people, Glasgow has been little more than a city passed through on the way north or south (sometimes east or west), but it is the superb focal point of a vast array of lovely scenery almost on its doorstep.

The more you explore with the aid of this book, the more you realise that Glasgow and its neighbourhood is a wonderful place to spend some time, a place to walk and to wonder.

All of the walks are roughly within a 30-mile (48-km) radius from Glasgow, the most far flung being Tinto, the highest summit in the Clyde Valley. One walk involves very little walking: Inchmahome in the lovely Lake of Menteith is the sort of place you need a small ferry boat to get to. Exploring takes only a short time, but the desire to leave is never pressing, so beautifully set is this small island.

Ferries are also needed to tackle the two walks I have included on the Island of Bute. One, from Kilchattan Bay, in all honesty ranks in the top ten walks from my lifetime of walking – maybe even in the top five. It was touch and go whether to include Bute, but, with good timing, a car-borne visitor can leave Glasgow and be in Rothesay in little more than an hour's driving.

Within the greater area of Glasgow there are walks through deep, wooded gorges, around huge 'boating' lakes, visiting stately homes,

Inchmahome Priory

country parks and outstanding museum collections. Farther afield, the lonely summit of Dungoil, in the Campsie Fells, is a simple pleasure, threading a way through woodlands populated with deer that gaze at you curiously before trotting out of sight, while buzzards mew at you from overhead. Below Auchineden Hill, the Whangie, a great cleft of rock said to be created by the Devil, has long been a popular weekend resort for Glaswegians, as has the lovely countryside surrounding Balloch Country Park at the southern end of Loch Lomond.

The Greenock Cut

Regrettably, Glasgow's 'own mountain' Ben Lomond, has had to be left out as being a little beyond the scope of this book: it was tempting to include it, but its ascent really is a strenuous business for anyone who is not a regular walker. But much of the countryside surrounding the Ben is explored – around Balmaha, Loch Lomond and Drymen – a good deal of which is now embraced in Scotland's first National Park – Loch Lomond and The Trossachs – declared in July 2002, just as this book was being researched.

Scotland is a country with a fascinating and intriguing history, and many of the people who were part of that history will be found in the pages that follow. But so will less celebrated people, and less well-known places. *Short Walks Glasgow* is about encounters with these people and places, and about the simple pleasures of walking in the countryside. Here there are countless opportunities to study birds, wild flowers and animals, or to watch patiently the coastal waters for passing dolphins, porpoises or whales. Simple field guides will help identify what you see, and, hopefully, encourage further exploration on your own – around Glasgow.

1 Inchmahome (Lake of Menteith)

START Port of Menteith
DISTANCE ½ mile (1km)
TIME 1 hour
PARKING Ferry point
ROUTE FEATURES Island paths, ferry crossing

Inchmahome Priory is one of Scotland's finest religious houses, and this ferry trip to explore its island takes visitors into another world – of peace and tranquillity. There is little descriptive walking to do, simply a gentle wander around the island and through the timeless buildings.

The ferry car park lies a short way down the B8034 **A**, and from here the ferryman needs to be summoned to cross from the island. The crossing, for which there is a charge, takes seven minutes, and is available from April until October, but may be cancelled in bad weather.

Once on the island, simply explore at leisure, or take a picnic to enjoy on the shores of the island. There is no need for a route description. ●

Inchmahome Priory, set on the largest of the three islands in Lake of Menteith, was founded in the 13th century for a small cell of Augustinian canons, and shortly before its dissolution, it hosted the infant Mary, Queen of Scots, who came to the island in 1547 for her safety.

Lake of Menteith is Scotland's only 'lake' as distinct from 'loch', and often freezes sufficiently to allow curling games to take place.

? *While crossing to and visiting the island, see how many different birds you can spot on the lake.*

PUBLIC TRANSPORT Buses along A81
REFRESHMENTS Port of Menteith and Aberfoyle
PUBLIC TOILETS Inchmahone
ORDNANCE SURVEY MAPS Explorer 365 (The Trossachs), Landranger 57 (Stirling & The Trossachs)

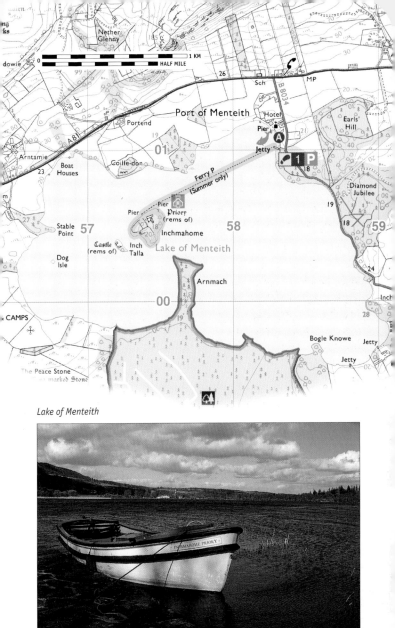

Lake of Menteith

Inchmahome Priory

Campsie Glen

START Clachan of Campsie
DISTANCE 1¼ miles (2km)
TIME 2 hours
PARKING Clachan of Campsie
ROUTE FEATURES Woodland trails, meadow paths

Rock and tree falls have caused the original route through Campsie Glen to be closed, for safety reasons. But the option remains to complete this walk in two parts, one exploring the glen, the other climbing to the upper reaches where more waterfalls await.

Before setting off up the glen, it is worth exploring the nearby graveyard at **St Machan's Church**, which also houses the mausoleum for the Lennox family, once a powerful force in this region.

Carved face: Campsie Glen

Begin by passing to the right of the buildings at Clachan, to gain a clear path striking up into Campsie Glen.

Walking up through the glen, keep an eye open for a variety of unexpected and unusual sculptures that dot the landscape – faces in trees, sheep, otters and fish for example.

PUBLIC TRANSPORT Buses to start
REFRESHMENTS Tea shop at start
PUBLIC TOILETS None on route
ORDNANCE SURVEY MAPS Explorer 348 (Campsie Fells), Landranger 64 (Glasgow)

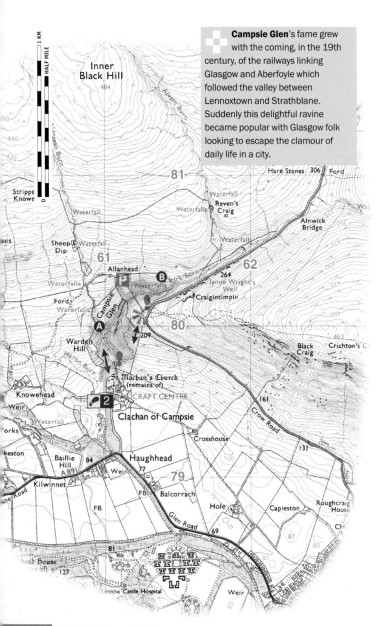

Campsie Glen's fame grew with the coming, in the 19th century, of the railways linking Glasgow and Aberfoyle which followed the valley between Lennoxtown and Strathblane. Suddenly this delightful ravine became popular with Glasgow folk looking to escape the clamour of daily life in a city.

The lower path climbs only as far as the waterfall known as James' Linn . From here, go back to the gate (sculpted sheep nearby), and there turn onto a steeply ascending path that climbs above the glen towards a higher car park with the opportunity to see more water-falls **B** with the delightful names Muckle Alicompen, Wee Alicompen and Sheep Linn.

Return by the same route, taking care on the descent if conditions are slippery underfoot.

See how many different sculptures you can find.

Heading into upper Campsie Glen

Waterfalls in upper Campsie Glen

3 *Balloch Castle*

START Castle Visitor Centre

DISTANCE 2 miles (3.2km)

TIME 1 hour

PARKING At start

ROUTE FEATURES Woodland trails, lochside paths, gentle uphill

This attractive country park within a short distance of Glasgow sits at the edge of one of Scotland's finest lochs. No monsters here, but the beauty of the area is legendary, and this easy stroll around the grounds of Balloch Castle a refreshing touch of escapism.

Begin from the car park (accessed via North Lodge along Mollanbowie Road in Balloch) and go down to visit the castle perched in a magnificent position overlooking the loch.

Continue past the castle and when the on-going drive forks, keep right and walk on to enter Moss o'Balloch Plantation.

Not long after entering the wooded area a broad track appears on the right **A**. Turn onto this and follow it to a bridge beyond which the track swings right, parallel with the River Leven and shortly reaching the banks of Loch Lomond itself.

The track widens as it approaches the loch, passing on the way a small flooded area on the right

The present-day **castle** was built in 1808 using stone from an earlier castle which had been the ancient residence of the earls of Lennox since the 13th century; it remained in the family until 1652 when it was bought by Sir John Colquhoun of Luss.

PUBLIC TRANSPORT Buses and trains to Balloch

REFRESHMENTS Visitor Centre and Balloch

PLAY AREA Near start

PUBLIC TOILETS At start

ORDNANCE SURVEY MAPS Explorer 347 (Loch Lomond South), Landranger 56 (Loch Lomond & Inveraray)

Balloch Castle

which provides an ideal habitat for amphibians and water-loving plants such as yellow iris.

Continue beside the lake, the path here flanked by substantial stands of beech, holly, rhododendron and sycamore.

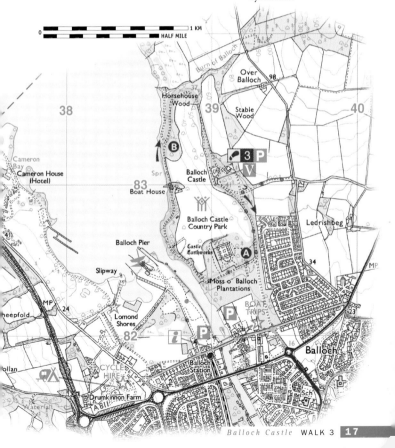

Loch Lomond is Britain's largest inland lake (by area), extending to 71 sq km; it is over 21 miles (34km) long and reaches depths of 525ft (190m). The loch has 38 islands, most of which are at the southern end, and is one of only two lochs where the freshwater fish, the 'powan', is found. More than 200 species of birds have been recorded around the loch, along with over 25 per cent of Britain's wild plants.

When the track forks, branch right , moving away from the lochside and into Horsehouse Wood, where the track now becomes surfaced and begins to climb gently.

Gradually, the path swings round to return to Balloch Castle. As the ascending path levels, there is a lovely view, right, across Loch Lomond to the wooded hillsides of Ben Bowie.

As you continue, you can see a noticeable difference in the range and planting of the trees and shrubbery around the castle: beech hedges are neatly trimmed, as are some of the ancient yews, and birch and rowan start to put in an appearance, too.

When the on-going track branches, keep forward, ignoring a right turn (which leads back to the castle). Instead, keep along the track to return to the car park. ●

Can you discover when Bran died?

Loch Lomond from Balloch Country Park

Balmaha and Craigie Fort

START	Balmaha
DISTANCE	2 miles (3km)
TIME	1 hour
PARKING	Balmaha
ROUTE FEATURES	Woodland paths and trails, steep ascents, very steep descent

4

The main feature of this short walk are the stunning viewpoints gained from two wooded rocky hillocks overlooking Balmaha. The walk is worth combining with a boat trip to the island of Inchcailloch, which can be arranged from Balmaha (the visitor centre has details).

Leave the car park and turn right, soon reaching the edge of Loch Lomond. Follow a concrete walkway alongside the water's edge until this emerges at a road junction. Ignore the main road bearing right, and, instead, go left.

About 100 yds (91m) along the road look for a waymark on the right marking the ascent of the West Highland Way onto a small hillock known as Craigie Fort. The view from the summit, northwards up Loch Lomond to Ben Lomond, is outstanding.

The **West Highland Way**, briefly shared by two sections of this walk, is an excellent middle-distance walk of 95 miles (152km) from the outskirts of Glasgow at Milngavie to Fort William. Its course spans the length of Loch Lomond in Glen Falloch and then on to Crianlarich. After Tyndrum it strikes across Rannoch Moor on the old Glencoe road before climbing over hills to Kinlochleven and a final stage through forest and into Glen Nevis.

Cross the summit and follow a descending path that zigzags down to meet another path (waymark) near the water's edge. Here, turn

PUBLIC TRANSPORT Buses to Balmaha
REFRESHMENTS Balmaha
PUBLIC TOILETS At start in visitor centre
ORDNANCE SURVEY MAPS Explorer 347 (Loch Lomond South), Landranger 56 (Loch Lomond & Inveraray)

left, and follow a shore path to a metal bridge not far from the pier serving the nearby island of Inchcailloch .

Beyond the bridge, turn left onto a road and follow this back to the concrete walkway used earlier. At a gap in the wall, cross the road with care and go up a path opposite (waymarked).

A short way beyond a waymark, the drainage ditch on the left is blocked by a small 'bridge' **B**. From here the walk climbs to another viewpoint. This time the climb is steep, and the descent even steeper, making this section unsuitable for very young children or anyone not confident on steep slopes. [*Anyone wanting to omit this section of the walk should simply keep forward along the*

Foxgloves growing in Balloch Country park

lower path, passing the turning into the Balmaha car park (a quick finish, if needed), and follow the track left to a blue-banded waymark near a small pond, where the higher option re-appears].

Loch Lomond from Craigie Fort

Otherwise, leave the path by crossing the ditch and climbing on a pine-needle path that rises steeply through bracken and foxgloves to reach a lovely viewpoint over the southern end of Loch Lomond.

Conic Hill is a significant landmark in geological terms because it lies directly on the Highland Boundary Fault, where the rugged terrain of Highland Scotland meets the softer sandstone landscape of the south.

From the viewpoint, continue climbing, more easily now, over two distinct rises to reach the high point of the walk and a good view to the north-east of shapely Conic Hill.

From the high point descend very steeply, with great care, especially if the ground is wet. Lower down, the difficulties ease as the path

> **?** See if you can find any evidence of the volcanoes that once were active here.

descends to the edge of a small pond.

A few strides farther on a broad path is encountered (near a blue-banded waymark: where the lower route is met). **C** Turn left on this, once more briefly using part of the West Highland Way.

The West Highland Way departs at the first turning on the left. Leave it, and continue ahead to a second turning, where the on-going track forks. Bear right, descending, and eventually reach a metal gate giving onto a surfaced driveway.

Walk out along the driveway to meet the main road, and there turn right to return to the starting point of the walk. ●

5 *Lunderston Bay*

START Lunderston Bay

DISTANCE 2½ miles (4.3km)

TIME 1–1½ hours

PARKING (along A770)

ROUTE FEATURES
Seashore paths, woodland trails, farm tracks

Lunderston Bay is part of the Clyde Muirshiel Regional Park, but only peripherally. Its main attribute is the taste it gives of the Clyde and the many to-ings and fro-ings that this major waterway supports. The range of wildlife is huge and this short walk could easily consume far more than the suggested time, especially if beachcombing comes into play.

Set off from the car park by heading left along the Clyde on a wide footpath that soon tacks closely along the high-tide line.

The path is a delight to follow, flanked by buttercups, red campion and a wide range of grasses, with shore birds such as ringed plover, greenshank, redshank, sandpiper dunlin and turnstone never far away.

Gradually, the path bends around a small promontory and finally approaches Ardgowan Point **A** where it enters Crowhill Wood.

Along the foreshore at Lunderston Bay

PUBLIC TRANSPORT Buses along A770

REFRESHMENTS Mobile snack bar at start

PUBLIC TOILETS Near start

PLAY AREA Near start

ORDNANCE SURVEY MAPS Explorer 341 (Greenock, Largs & Millport), Landranger 63 (Firth of Clyde)

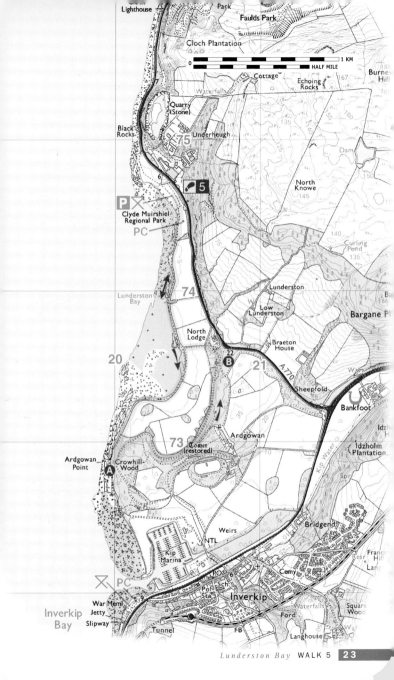

Lunderston Bay

Just on entering the wood, bear left to intercept a broad woodland track. Turn left along this track and follow it for about ³⁄₄ of a mile (1.4km) until it rises (passing a cottage) to meet another track at a T-junction **B**.

Turn left along the track, keep ahead at another junction, passing North Lodge on the right, and shortly, when the track forks, branch left and walk down a field edge towards the Clyde.

In the bottom corner of the field, pass through a gate and turn right, rejoining the outward route, which should be retraced back to the starting point of the walk. ●

The **Clyde** is popular with a wide range of sea birds, most notably eider, that gather in large 'rafts', oystercatcher, that patrol the water's edge, and gannets that fly up and down in search of a snack to drop in on. Keep an eye open for clusters of shattered muscle shells: these tell you where oystercatchers have been having lunch.

? *Can you spot any seals?*

Chatelherault Country Park

6

START Chatelherault
DISTANCE 2¾ miles (4.5km)
TIME 1½ hours
PARKING At country park
ROUTE FEATURES Woodland trails, riverside paths, short steep ascent and descent

The delightful Avon Water lies completely out of sight and sound of the urban sprawl of Glasgow, giving this short walk popular appeal. In spite of this, it is easy to wander the woodlands peacefully and to enjoy the country park that surrounds this splendid hunting lodge on the outskirts of Hamilton.

Walk up to the visitor centre and, in front of it, turn left on a descending path (signposted to Duke's Bridge). Follow the track to a junction, turning left to reach the bridge.

Over the bridge the route bears

In Chatelherault Country Park

Chatelherault is fundamentally a hunting lodge, dog kennel and summer palace commissioned by the 5th Duke of Hamilton. It was later transformed into one of Scotland's greatest stately homes in the early 1800s by the 10th Duke.

PUBLIC TRANSPORT Buses pass entrance to country park
REFRESHMENTS Restaurant at visitor centre
PLAY AREA Near car park
PUBLIC TOILETS In visitor centre
ORDNANCE SURVEY MAPS Explorer 343 (Motherwell & Coatbridge), Landranger 64 (Glasgow)

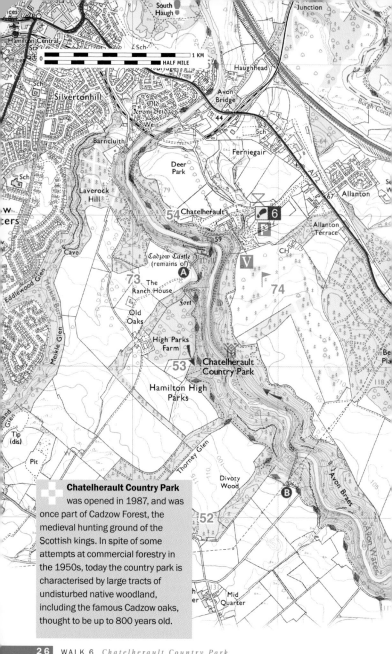

Chatelherault Country Park

was opened in 1987, and was once part of Cadzow Forest, the medieval hunting ground of the Scottish kings. In spite of some attempts at commercial forestry in the 1950s, today the country park is characterised by large tracts of undisturbed native woodland, including the famous Cadzow oaks, thought to be up to 800 years old.

Chatelherault

B Just after passing beneath overhead power-lines and by a bench, leave the main track by branching left onto a descending flight of steps made up of bricks. This leads down to White Bridge.

Over the bridge, continue to a path junction, and there follow the sign for Chatelherault. The path soon begins to descend steeply and once more runs parallel with the river. When the on-going track forks, branch right, climbing above the river to meet a broad track.

Cross the track and go up steps opposite, following a wall to an entrance gateway. Turn in and immediately right to pass through the attractive gardens of Chatelherault, and soon return to the visitor centre.

right around Cadzow Castle, and later swings left and runs up to a gate and cattle grid **A**. Just before the gate, turn left on a grassy path (signposted to White Bridge). This shortly joins a main track. Bear right.

The track wanders on through mixed woodland of larch, beech, birch, ash, sycamore, and elm, and features an abundance of wild flowers from wild garlic to buttercup, wood sorrel and herb robert.

The path does a loop around a narrow glen, escaping by a brief, steep climb shortly to swing into a more open area and passing a small reedy pond before returning to woodland.

> **?** *Pied wagtails are fairly common in country parks, but see if you can spot any grey wagtails that favour riversides.*

7 *Mugdock*

START Mugdock Country Park Visitor Centre

DISTANCE 2¾ miles (4.4km)

TIME 1½ hours

PARKING Visitor Centre

ROUTE FEATURES Woodland trails, lakeside paths

Mugdock astounds, there is so much of interest in such a compact area. Not surprisingly, the country park is popular throughout the year, and has all the facilities anyone needs. Although this walk makes a satisfactory tour of the park, there is much to commend a longer stay and further independent exploration.

Head towards the visitor centre (which also houses toilets, an interpretation centre, a shop and small café), and on the other side take the track signposted to Gallow Hill. Almost immediately, bear right to pass the Wildlife Garden and follow a gently

In the 19th century, a pool on **Gallow Hill** provided a water supply for the nearby Craigend Castle, but for more than a hundred years it was the local place of execution. Women found guilty could expect to be drowned in the pool, men would be hanged from the gibbet, or gallows.

Swan and cygnet, Mugdock Country Park

descending path around the base of Gallow Hill.

Continue to reach the ruins of Craigend Castle **A**, an early example of Scottish Gothic Revival

PUBLIC TRANSPORT Buses from Milngavie (summer only)

REFRESHMENTS Café in visitor centre

PUBLIC TOILETS Near visitor centre

ORDNANCE SURVEY MAPS Explorer 348 (Campsie Fells), Landranger 64 (Glasgow)

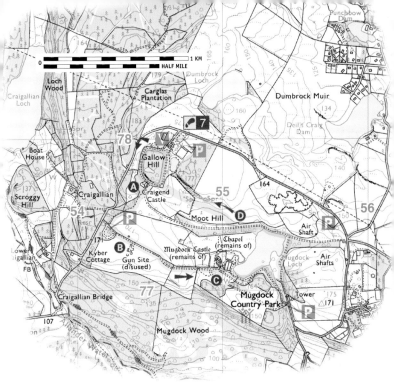

architecture, built in 1816 after the demise of John Smith, the 4th laird of Craigend.

Turn in front of the castle and shortly branch right onto a path signposted for the Khyber Car Park. The path undulates agreeably as it passes through a neck of mixed woodland of sycamore, ash, birch and larch and finally rises gently to meet a path near the car park. Through a gate turn left (signposted for Mugdock Castle).

Continue through another gate and follow the on-going track, passing some patently derelict but curious brick structures. These are gun emplacements **B** used during the Second World War to defend Glasgow and the Clyde.

Keep ahead across fields and then into an avenue of trees, through a gate and on to reach Mugdock Castle **C**.

After a brief tour of the castle walk past it, with Mugdock Loch soon coming into view. Stay with the main track as it bends left to run

Mugdock Castle

Mugdock Castle was the seat of one of Scotland's most important noble families, the Grahams, from the 13th century until the 20th. Sir John de Graham was of key importance in William Wallace's campaign for the independence of Scotland, while James Graham was a close ally of Rob Roy MacGregor.

alongside the loch, and then later move away from it.

At a signpost turn left over a footbridge, heading back towards the visitor centre. At the next junction, go left again, around the edge of the lake.

Keep following a wide track as far as a distinct branching path on the right **D**. Here, leave the main track and walk up onto grassy moorland dotted with birch and willow and harbouring a wide range of grasses and grassland flowers like speedwell, buttercup, lesser stitchwort, foxglove and common spotted orchid.

The path shortly follows the course of overhead powerlines, and runs on to meet another. Go forward onto a gravel path and follow this, bearing right, to reach another smaller lake.

Keep to the left of the lake and soon return to the visitor centre. ●

? *Kestrels can often be seen hovering above the countryside. See how many you can spot on this walk.*

Bogany Wood

START Rothesay (Bute)
DISTANCE 3 miles (5km)
TIME 1½ hours
PARKING Rothesay (Pay and Display)
ROUTE FEATURES Woodland trails, roads, steep, winding descent

8

Bogany Wood, also known as Skipper Wood, occupies the headland above Rothesay, overlooking the Firth of Clyde. This mature woodland offers an easy and delightful walk with numerous cameos of the Clyde, the Kyles of Bute and the Cowal Peninsula. It finishes with a spectacular serpentine descent.

Set off from the car park opposite the turning onto the pier by walking across Watergate and into West Princes Street, and at its end turn right into East Princes Street. Walk as far as Castle Street and there turn left into a steep road set in zigzags, previously known as Mount Pleasant but now, seemingly, Serpentine Road.

Use steps on the left, and at the top take the first left (Bishop Terrace). A short way along the terrace, at a signpost, branch left into Skipper Wood **A**.

The zigzagging Serpentine Road, back into Rothesay

PUBLIC TRANSPORT Bus and rail to Wemyss Bay, ferry to Rothesay
REFRESHMENTS Rothesay
PUBLIC TOILETS Quayside, Rothesay
ORDNANCE SURVEY MAPS Explorer 362 (Cowal West & Isle of Bute), Landranger 63 (Firth of Clyde)

A terraced path flanked by a wall hosting ivy-leaved toadflax, moss and ferns leads into the woodland above the harbour.

When the path forks, branch right, staying on the main path, which continues across a footbridge and through a well-established broad-leaved woodland of beech, ash, rhododendron, birch, willow and sycamore.

> **?** *Look for some examples of coppicing, the traditional craft of stimulating new growth by pruning trees close to the ground.*

Just after a barrier, when the path forks again, keep right, passing delightful views of the Clyde and the Kyles of Bute.

At a road **B**, turn right and walk

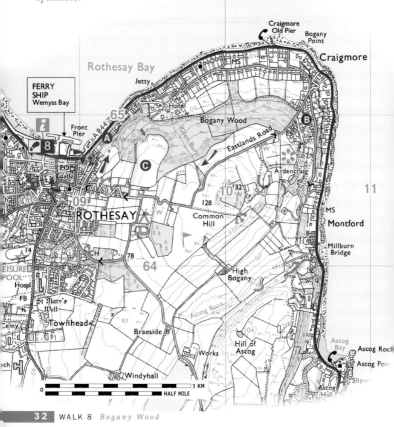

Bogany Wood is a backdrop to the harbour at Rothesay

up past the entrance to Ardencraig Gardens and Aviaries. Continue to an S-bend, and there leave the road by turning onto a signposted bridleway for Serpentine Road.

The on-going bridleway is a pleasure to follow. It loops around a large open pasture, where deer can sometimes be spotted, and finally leads to a wooden gate **C**.

Through the gate, turn right and walk along a field edge to another gate and a path beyond leading between houses and out to the top of Serpentine Road.

Serpentine Road now lives up to its

Rothesay Castle, surrounded by a moat, was used as a royal palace by Robert III, having earlier been besieged by Vikings. The castle was finally destroyed in the 17th century, and although there has been some restoration work, it remains largely a ruin.

name as it descends in a series of zigzags back towards Rothesay. For pedestrians, the zigzags are eased by a more direct flight of steps. At the bottom, go forward into Castle Street.

At Rothesay Castle, turn right into High Street and walk down to the seafront and the conclusion of the walk. ●

9 *South Calder Water*

START Strathclyde Country Park
DISTANCE 3 miles (5km)
TIME 1½ hours
PARKING Car park at Bothwellhaugh Plantation
ROUTE FEATURES Woodland trails, riverside paths

So compelling are the attractions of the nearby Strathclyde Country Park that few visitors venture along the in-flowing South Calder Water. Here, amid broad-leaved trees, are meadows full of wild flowers and alive with birdsong, through which the river ambles peacefully.

Leave the car park by heading towards the toilet block, and walk up a flight of steps, turning right at the top along a wooded pathway.

Go forward across a footbridge and soon reach a road, near a roundabout. Cross the road and walk up more steps opposite, continuing as far as the first path on the left.

Here, turn back into woodland on a gently ascending path above South Calder Water that wanders through delightful woodlands of hawthorn, ash, beech, young chestnut, sycamore, oak and elm before breaking out into a more open area near a children's play area.

Bear right to pass the play area and then take the next turning on the left, near a bench, to walk alongside a golf course **A**.

When the path next forks, bear right, descending to a large clear area. Follow the path to its end at a turning circle, and there go forward into woodland on an

PUBLIC TRANSPORT Buses to entrance of park
PLAY AREA Along the walk
PUBLIC TOILETS At start
ORDNANCE SURVEY MAPS Explorer 343 (Motherwell & Coatbridge), Landranger 64 (Glasgow)

undulating path that now stays close to the river.

The path eventually comes down to the side of the river, passing below a line of cliffs and then a very tall railway viaduct.

Heath spotted orchid along South Calder Water

Continue through more woodland to another clearer area of grassland bright in summer with a wide range of flowers that include comfrey, speedwell, buttercup and cranesbill.

Meadow cranesbill

At a bridge the path is deflected upwards **B**. Turn right to cross the bridge and 100 yds (91m) farther on, turn right onto a broad track that begins the return leg of the walk.

Ignore a branching path on the left, and keep descending to rejoin the river near a weir.

The path later climbs a flight of steps. At the top, turn right and keep right a few strides later to tackle yet more steps. This time the path goes forward, high above the river, and flanked by beech, rowan, sycamore, oak, hawthorn and birch.

Once again, the path passes beneath the railway viaduct, but this time rather nearer the top. The

The Roman fort alongside South Calder Water

Rotten trees make an ideal habitat for fungi, wild flowers, mosses and lichens

path, which is a delight to follow, steadily moves away from the river and approaches a small modern housing estate.

Follow the path along the edge of the housing estate and then across grassland to join a surfaced path, bearing right past a school playing field **C**.

The path finally emerges at a road. Cross to the footpath opposite and turn right. The on-going path stays roughly parallel with the road and

See if you can find another word for forest or woodland on this walk.

The bathhouse is associated with a fort that stood a little to the south, a day's march from the **Antonine Wall**, a later, less substantial and less enduring version of Hadrian's Wall. The fort garrison was about 500 strong, men who belonged to the Auxilia, which means that they were probably drawn from various outposts of the Roman Empire.

leads down to the site of a Roman Military Bathhouse.

Cross a nearby footbridge and walk to a path junction. Turn right and cross the nearby road, on the other side joining the outward route. Turn left and follow the path back to the car park.

10 Pollok Country Park

START Pollokshaws
DISTANCE 3 miles (5km)
TIME 1½ hours
PARKING Near Pollok House (Free)
ROUTE FEATURES Parkland trails, riverside paths, woodland

Pollok Country Park must be unique in boasting not just woodland and acres of open parkland, but two important art collections, in Pollok House and the Burrell Museum. This walk visits both, enabling visitors to make the trip last a whole day.

Walk from the car park towards Pollok House, pass through an archway and walk round to the front of the house. (A visit is recommended. The house is truly fascinating.)

Continue past the front of the house and turn right through an adjoining garden to reach the gardens fronting the river. Walk along the driveway to a river, White Cart Water. Turn left.

Follow a broad track towards another group of buildings – the

The Maxwell family is known to have lived at **Pollok** in the 13th century. The present house dates from 1750 and replaces three earlier buildings. It was extended in 1890 by Sir John Stirling Maxwell, a founder member of the National Trust for Scotland. The house contains an internationally important collection of paintings, silver and ceramics, and visitors can have a taste of life in an Edwardian kitchen, now converted to an excellent restaurant/café.

old stables courtyard **A**, and there walk between the buildings and continue forward along a

PUBLIC TRANSPORT Buses into country park
REFRESHMENTS Café in Pollok House and Burrell Museum
PUBLIC TOILETS Pollok House
ORDNANCE SURVEY MAPS Explorer 342 (Glasgow), Landranger 64 (Glasgow)

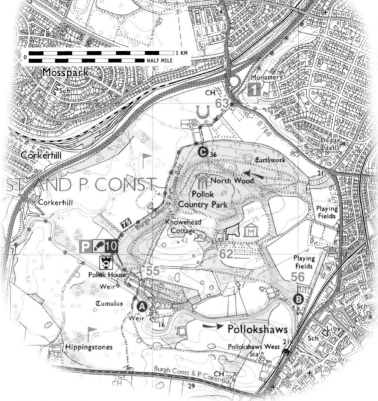

The river at Pollok

surfaced driveway flanked on the right by a tall beech hedgerow.

When the hedge ends, the on-going drive runs alongside the river. Where it forks, bear right and eventually go past open pastures, a cricket ground and tennis courts to meet the main driveway **B**.

Turn left for a short distance and then leave the main drive by branching right on a woodland

Pollok House from the river entrance

path signposted to the Burrell Collection.

At the museum, go forward past Knowehead Lodge and a few strides farther on bear right and take the right-hand one of two driveways, then going forward, ascending slightly.

When the track next divides, bear right along a woodland driveway flanked by ewe, rhododendron,

The Burrell Collection contains more than 8,000 art objects amassed during the lifetime of Sir William Burrell, a Glasgow shipping magnate. It is housed in a purpose-built building, and is a unique and outstanding collection.

Can you find any lions?

beech and ash. The track later bends left, becoming stony and climbing gently into North Wood. A short way on, it bends right, and then after about 300 yds (273m) forks again. Branch left and immediately left again along the broader of two tracks that eventually passes a pond and soon merges with a surfaced driveway **C**.

Remain on the surfaced driveway, ignoring branching tracks, and eventually the track leads round to a barrier on the main driveway near Pollok House. Turn right to return to the car park.

Strathclyde Country Park

START Bothwellhaugh Pavilion
DISTANCE 4 miles (6.3km)
TIME 2 hours
PARKING Bothwellhaugh
ROUTE FEATURES Woodland trails, lakeside paths

11

Strathclyde Country Park is one of the most popular visitor attractions in Britain, and deservedly so. It caters for everyone and positively exudes the sense of well-being that comes from being in the open air, whether jogging, walking, cycling or just watching everyone else.

Begin from the car park near the visitor centre and walk down the access road, going through a metal barrier to reach the lake edge. Turn right.

Follow the lochside path, and when it forks branch left **A**, staying alongside the loch. Far to the south, the domed summit of Tinto, the highest point in the

How many different kinds of boat can you see on the loch?

Strathclyde Loch is man-made and, having an international standard rowing course that was used for the 1986 Commonwealth Games, is used by the National Rowing Academy, as well as people with less demanding water-based ambitions.

Clyde Valley, sits hazily on the horizon (*See Walk 15*).

Keep going past the boathouse and eventually emerge onto a road. Bear left (there is a footpath on the opposite side of the road), and walk round the end of the loch,

PUBLIC TRANSPORT Buses to entrance of park
REFRESHMENTS Within park
PICNIC AREAS At start and on far side of loch
PLAY AREA Various, including fun fair
PUBLIC TOILETS At boathouse
ORDNANCE SURVEY MAPS Explorer 343 (Motherwell & Coatbridge), Landranger 64 (Glasgow)

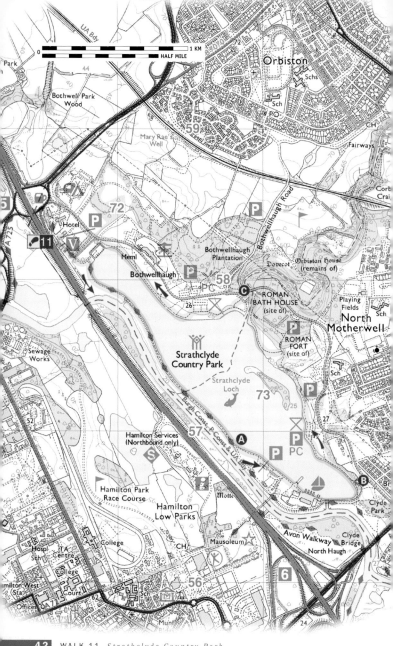

Gathering of swans at Strathclyde Country Park

then return to a lochside path **B**. The path soon passes a wide, sandy bay (near a car park, picnic spot and play area) and then enters an area of waterside shrubbery which hosts a wide range of shrubs, grasses and wild flowers.

When the path forks, bear right, climbing and descending a little through an area much-favoured by wildflowers, especially orchids.

Eventually, the path encounters in-flowing South Calder Water and is deflected to the right where it reaches the remains of a Roman Military Bathhouse **C**, (*which is detailed in* Walk 9 South Calder Water).

Sailing on Strathclyde Water

Just after the bath-house, go left over a footbridge. At a path junction, take the second left towards the loch. There, bear right and follow the lochside path back to meet the outward route. Turn right and pass the visitor centre to the start. ●

12 The Whangie and Auchineden Hill

START A809, Queens' View

DISTANCE 4 miles (6.7km)

TIME 2 hours

PARKING Queen's View.

ROUTE FEATURES Moorland paths, boggy ground, rock outcrops

Auchineden Hill and the adjacent rock cleft known as The Whangie have long been a popular weekend jaunt. They are accessible without too much difficulty and yet still offer a sense of remoteness, especially looking southwards across the moors to Burncrooks Reservoir.

🥾 The car park at the start of the walk is itself a very good vantage point, but leave it along a paved path to a low stile beyond which old railway sleepers 'pave' a way across a short stretch of marshy ground (a

View from near the summit of Auchineden Hill

good place to find common spotted orchids) before a good path rises steeply alongside nearby woodland.

The path climbs steadily to a ladder stile after which it takes a more gentle line as if to encourage visitors to spend time taking in the

PUBLIC TRANSPORT Buses along A809

REFRESHMENTS Drymen

PUBLIC TOILETS None

ORDNANCE SURVEY MAPS Explorer 347 (Loch Lomond South), Landranger 56 (Loch Lomond & Inveraray)

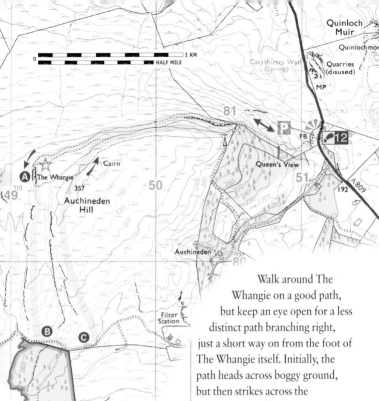

view northwards to Loch Lomond and the distinctive knobbly summit of Ben Lomond.

When the ongoing path forks, bear right on a good path that gradually works a way round to the rocky outcrop, fissured it is said by a whimsical crack of the Devil's tail, known as The Whangie ('whangie' being a Scottish word for a slice), and looking exactly as though it has been sliced from the outcrop **A**.

Walk around The Whangie on a good path, but keep an eye open for a less distinct path branching right, just a short way on from the foot of The Whangie itself. Initially, the path heads across boggy ground, but then strikes across the moorland roughly heading for Burncrooks Reservoir. The path improves as it goes, and follows the edge of a low escarpment.

Gradually, the moorland path descends to intercept a rough-surfaced reservoir access track **B**. Turn left onto this and soon pass a gated turning into Auchineden Plantation. Go past this, a little farther, to a gateless opening on the right.

C Leave the main track by

turning left onto a narrow grassy path (directly opposite the opening) that treks back across the moorland, but this time heading directly for the top of Auchineden Hill. The area around the access track is a good place to keep an eye open for adders which can often be seen warming themselves on rocks and grassy bumps – so, be careful where you sit.

The top of Auchineden Hill is marked by a trig pillar. From it head for a clear path (protected by a ring of boggy ground) that leads across the hill, descending slightly to the left, improving as it goes.

Eventually, the descending path rejoins the lower path to The Whangie used on the outward section, and this should be followed back to the start.

? *Can you find the number 36 followed by the number 38?*

On the summit of Auchineden Hill

Drymen and Buchanan Castle

13

Easy walking initially around farmland north of Drymen leads to a visit to the Buchanan Estate and its ruined castle. There are numerous viewpoints that embrace Loch Lomond and its islands as well as the valley of Endrick Water.

START Drymen
DISTANCE 4¼ miles (6.8km)
TIME 2 hours
PARKING Drymen: Stirling Road car park (Free)
ROUTE FEATURES Farmland, woodland, estate roads

Leave the Stirling Road car park and walk left towards the road junction at The Square, and there turn right, going past the Clachan Inn. Walk up into Old Gartmore Road and keep on to pass Drymen Primary School, just after which the distinctive knobbly shape of Conic Hill comes into view on the left.

Continue as far as a turning on the left between gate pillars at Coldrach Lodge (West Highland Way waymark nearby). **A** Leave the road here by turning onto a rough track that rises very gently and proves a lovely viewpoint northwards to Loch Lomond and its islands, before descending equally gently to pass Coldrach Farm.

At a T-junction near the edge of a plantation, turn left and follow a track out to meet the B837 at Buchanan Smithy. Turn right

? *The woodlands and fields around Drymen are attractive to buzzards. See if you can spot or hear any?*

PUBLIC TRANSPORT Buses to Drymen
REFRESHMENTS Pubs and hotels in Drymen
PUBLIC TOILETS None on route
ORDNANCE SURVEY MAPS Explorer 347 (Loch Lomond South), Landranger 56 (Loch Lomond & Inveraray)

The cottages adjoining **Buchanan Smithy** were once occupied by workers on the Buchanan Estate and date from the early 18th century.

passing the terraced rows of Buchanan Smithy Cottages.

Just before reaching the last cottage, leave the B-road by turning left down a narrow track. Continue to reach the edge of woodland. Go forward for about 100 yds (91m), to an obvious cross track. Here, turn left **B**.

After about 200 yds (183m), at a road junction, turn left on an ascending surfaced lane (ignore the signposted route to Drymen), and walk up the lane as far as the

Conic Hill from near Buchanan Smithy

turning to Rohallion. There, turn right towards the ruins of Buchanan Castle **C**, now visible ahead, and wend a way between modern houses to reach it.

> **Buchanan Castle** was built in the 1850s, and was used as a military hospital during the Second World War. It was here that Hitler's deputy, Rudolf Hess, was taken in 1942 after his flight from Germany the previous year.

Walk away from the castle down a straight driveway, following this (*taking care against approaching traffic heading to and from the Buchanan Castle Golf Course*) for a little under a mile (1.4km) to meet the A811. On the way there are some lovely views over Strathendrick.

Cross to the roadside footpath opposite and turn left, and shortly turn into the side road leading back to Drymen. ●

Buchanan Castle

14 *Kilchattan*

START Kilchattan (Bute)
DISTANCE 4½ miles (7.3km)
TIME 2–2½ hours
PARKING Kilchattan
ROUTE FEATURES Seashore path, hill paths, farm tracks, undulating farmland, woodland

One of the most agreeable and satisfying short walks anywhere in Britain, this outstanding circuit visits the southern end of Bute, courting the coast as far as Glencallum Bay before heading inland to a jewel of a loch and the atmospheric ruins of St Blane's Chapel.

Set off from the jetty in Kilchattan Bay and follow the road past the last house where it narrows and leads to the start of the West Island Way, a 30-mile (48-km) walk along the length of the island.

A gated path, sometimes on a boardwalk, leads around the coast to the conspicuous crags of Hawk's Nib **A**, so named because the cliffs resemble the beak of a bird. Across the firth lie the islands of Great and Little Cumbrae.

Below Hawk's Nib the path is both undulating and, rocky, and, for a short while, demands extra care and attention.

Beyond Hawk's Nib the path becomes grassy once more, passing through bracken as it heads for the lighthouse at Rubh' an Eun and the dark volcanic sands of Glencallum Bay. Farther out to sea rise the distinctive shapes of Arran, Holy Island and, beyond them, the towering grey rock cone of Ailsa Craig.

PUBLIC TRANSPORT Bus or rail to Wemyss Bay, ferry to Rothesay, bus to Kilchattan

REFRESHMENTS Hotels in Kilchattan and Kingarth

PUBLIC TOILETS Near jetty

ORDNANCE SURVEY MAPS Explorer 362 (Cowal West & Isle of Bute), Landranger 63 (Firth of Clyde)

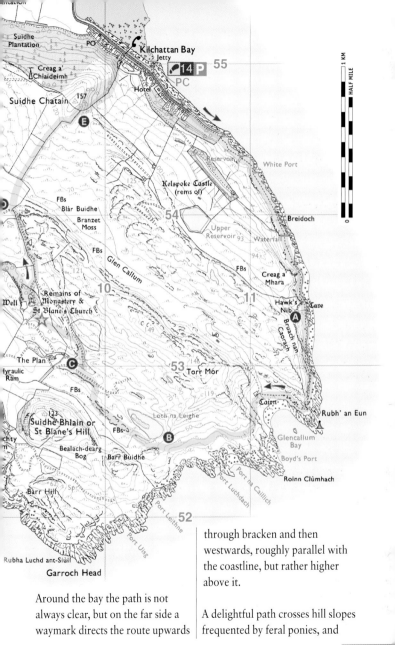

Around the bay the path is not always clear, but on the far side a waymark directs the route upwards

through bracken and then westwards, roughly parallel with the coastline, but rather higher above it.

A delightful path crosses hill slopes frequented by feral ponies, and

St Blane's Chapel

descending to intercept a farm track, not far from The Plan .

Walk towards the farm, but soon leave the track by turning right at a signpost for the West Island Way and Suidhe Chatain. A grassy path cuts across to another farm track. Turn right on this for a short distance to another signpost for St Blane's.

leads to a shallow pass between low hills **B**. Below, set in a hollow lies the reed-lined, lily-covered Loch na Leighe, a jewel among the hills, popular with swans. To the left rises the rugged Suidhe Bhlain (St Blane's Hill).

Go past the first pass to the next, through which the on-going path takes a course, descending steadily to a waymark. More waymarks now guide the route through brackeny undulations, finally

Leave the track here by turning left onto a rising grassy path through bracken that leads to a ladder-stile. Over this, strike out into the ensuing pasture, heading for a distant waymark.

From the waymark head for a step-stile spanning a fence and then walk up towards the ruins of St Blane's Chapel.

Continue past the chapel and head for a gap in the boundary wall (Vallum), then go forward on a broad grassy path to a gate giving onto a farm track. Turn left along this.

Follow the track to its end, climbing gently. Across its high

St Blane was born in the 6th century and educated in Ireland, returning to Kingarth as a young man. He was one of the earliest Scottish missionaries and established Christian communities elsewhere in Scotland, notably at Dunblane and Strathblane. In 788, Vikings raided Bute and burned the church and monastery. The church was rebuilt in Norman times.

point, descend to a step-stile over a fence **D**, and from this bear half-right in the ensuing pasture, heading downhill, targeting the rounded lump of Suidhe Chatain. When a metal gate comes into view, head for this.

Go up the next field with a fence on the right, continuing across stiles and up more fields to a point where the fence dog-legs right to a gate **E** immediately below the grassy slopes of Suidhe Chatain. A brief diversion to the top of the hill will provide a stunning panorama of virtually the whole of Bute, and farther afield to Arran, the Cowal Peninsula and the mainland.

Through the gate go left, down to another waymark and then turn onto a grassy path, descending towards Kilchattan Bay. The path leads to a narrow gate. Go through this and continue to descend, now beside a wall.

The descending path is steep and very slippery in places, and requires care, especially after rain.

Keep an eye open for a gate and waymark on the left. Turn through this into woodland, where the path, still slippery, continues descending, finally to emerge at the back of the seafront properties in Kilchattan.

Walk between the houses to the road and turn right to complete the walk. ●

Looking across to Arran from Kilchattan walk

? *The coastal waters around Bute are frequented by gannets, large white birds with black wing tips, renowned for plummeting into the sea to catch fish. See how many you can spot.*

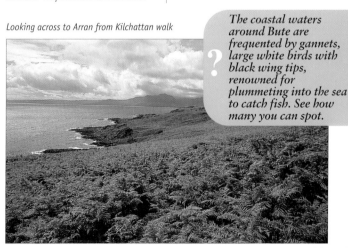

15 *Tinto*

Tinto is the highest summit in the Clyde Valley and its ascent is a generally uncomplicated if energetic affair. Almost entirely encircled by the Clyde and its tributaries, Tinto holds a sentinel position above the Clyde.

START Thankerton

DISTANCE 4½ miles (7km)

HEIGHT GAIN 1,558 feet (475m)

TIME 2–2½ hours

PARKING Car park at Fallburn

ROUTE FEATURES Mountain tracks, steep ascent and descent, exposed summit

Leave the car park and go through a nearby gate beyond which an enclosed track leads to another gate and a ladder-stile.

Ahead, Totherin Hill, the northern guardian of Tinto, rises steadily. Beyond the ladder-stile continue on a broad and obvious track.

Continue past the hill fort, climbing steadily onto Totherin Hill Ⓐ where the gradient eases for a while. A level stretch ensues, with the summit of Tinto Hill now in view.

Tinto from the Culter Fells

PUBLIC TRANSPORT Buses to Thankerton

REFRESHMENTS Tea shop at A73 crossroads

PUBLIC TOILETS None on route

ORDNANCE SURVEY MAPS Explorer 335 (Lanark & Tinto Hills), Landranger 72 (Upper Clyde Valley)

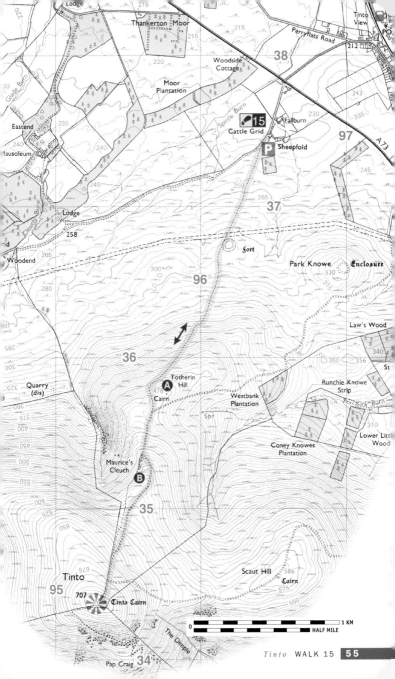

Ascending Tinto at Maurice's Cleuch

Above Totherin Hill the path passes above Maurice's Cleuch **B**, a steep ravine of shale, scree and heather.

Keep above the edge of Maurice's Cleuch and press on to meet a fence which is now followed all the way to the summit.

The summit of Tinto is marked by

Beside the track stands the **Fallburn Iron Age hill fort**, one of about thirty in the former county of Lanarkshire, all dating from the first millennium BC. The fort at Fallburn is almost circular with double ramparts and ditches, built first to defend against marauding neighbours and later against the forces of Rome.

Archaeological finds have shown that **Tinto** was a site of worship and burial by ancient tribes, a prospect greatly enhanced by the summit's domination of the surrounding farmlands.

an enormous pile of stones into which has been fashioned a circular stone shelter and an orientation table.

Return to the start by the outward route, *taking great care on the steeper sections.*

?
See how many of the distant hill groups you can see from the summit.

Dungoil

16

START Near Fintry
DISTANCE 4¾ miles (7.6km)
TIME 2 hours
PARKING Lay-by near start
ROUTE FEATURES Woodland trails, hill paths

This out-and-back walk visits a broad grassy summit high above Strathendrick over which it has unrivalled views that embrace a sizeable wedge of the Campsie Fells. The route is very simple, and the way enlivened by glimpses of deer, and buzzards mewing overhead.

Begin the walk at a gate about a mile (1.6km) south of the junction between the B822 and B818 (the lay-by is a short way farther south), and beyond the gate follow a broad track striking across the slopes of Dungoil, which looms above.

At another gate, enter the forest on a gently ascending track between mature stands of spruce.

After a little over 1¼ miles (2km) the track swings left and rises to a junction. Keep left **A**.

There are two contenders for the highest point of **Dungoil**, but that on the left claims the title. From it, the starting point comes into view, but it is the stunning panorama of hills near and far that is the highlight of this simple walk.

The track divides again about 200 yds (183m) farther on. Once more keep left and soon pass a small loch on the right, largely reed filled.

A little more than 100 yds (91m) beyond the lochan, a small cleared area appears on the left **B**: fire

PUBLIC TRANSPORT None of any use
REFRESHMENTS Pub near Fintry, or Lennoxtown
PUBLIC TOILETS None on route
ORDNANCE SURVEY MAPS Explorer 348 (Campsie Fells), Landranger 57 (Stirling & The Trossachs)

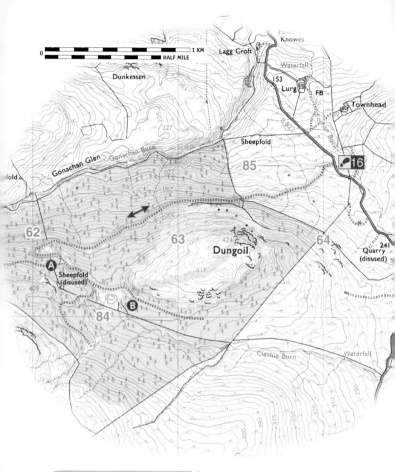

> *The forest is a favourite haunt of roe deer. See if you can spot any.*

warning signs and beaters mark the spot. Here, leave the main trail and head to the left corner of the cleared area where it is possible to pass through what turns out to be a narrow neck of forest (it seems

much more substantial from the track).

On the other side, go right to pass steeply around a low rocky outcrop above which a clear grassy path leads onwards across the top of the hill, where bog cotton is an abundant indicator of wet going (although the path is largely dry).

Dungoil

Do not be drawn into attempting a beeline descent for the starting point: such a course is fraught with difficulty and danger in the form of rocky outcrops, forest and steep grassy slopes.

Simply retrace the outward route. At the low outcrop (best passed at the forest edge on the left), the route back through the trees is marked by a small group of boulders.

●

Strathendrick from the track to Dungoil

17 Aberfoyle and Lochan Spling

START Aberfoyle
DISTANCE 5 miles (8.2km)
TIME 2–2½ hours
PARKING Aberfoyle
ROUTE FEATURES
Woodland trails, lakeside paths

The attraction of this walk comes simply from the pleasure of wandering along wide woodland trails taking in the flora and fauna and enjoying the views. Spring brings a host of flowers and birds; winter brings snow and a silence that is eerie.

Begin from the car park in Aberfoyle and walk out to cross the narrow bridge spanning the River Forth. Walk past modern housing and take the turning signposted to the Covenanters Inn. Walk up past the hotel, and keep forward into the edge of the Loch Ard Forest.

The track runs arrow-straight into the forest. After about half a mile (800m), at a staggered cross track **A**, turn right, following waymarks banded with yellow and blue.

There is a tendency to think that forests such as this are dank, lifeless places, but the reality is that this is an excellent habitat for a wide range of flowers and a host of birds such as **warblers**, members of the tit family, **thrushes**, **blackbirds**, **buzzards** and **kestrels**.

A short way farther on, at another junction, bear left, keeping to the lower of two paths, and soon reach the wooded Lochan Spling, often so still it faithfully mirrors the surrounding trees.

Continue in the company of the lochan (a small loch) for a while

PUBLIC TRANSPORT Buses to Aberfoyle
REFRESHMENTS Aberfoyle
PUBLIC TOILETS None on route
ORDNANCE SURVEY MAPS Explorer 365 (The Trossachs), Landranger 57 (Stirling & The Trossachs)

before the track turns away to effect a wide loop, that eventually reaches a T-junction **B** where the blue-banded and yellow-banded trails separate. [*Anyone wanting to shorten the walk, should turn left here and follow the yellow trail back to the entrance to the forest.*]

Track through Aberfoyle Forest

Otherwise, turn right, once more on a broad trail occasionally used by vehicles.

At Gartnaul, two renovated cottages mark the point of return. Here, take a gently rising track opposite the cottages, following this as it climbs the flanks of Garbeg Hill.

Once the track starts to descend, keep following it as far as a blue waymark on the left **C**, and here leave the main track by turning down a narrow trail that weaves a way downwards to meet a broad trail below, near Lochan Spling.

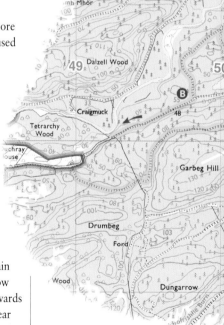

Turn right and follow the trail to the staggered junction encountered near the start of the walk, and keep forward to retrace the outward route back to Aberfoyle. ●

See how many different species of birds you can spot on this walk.

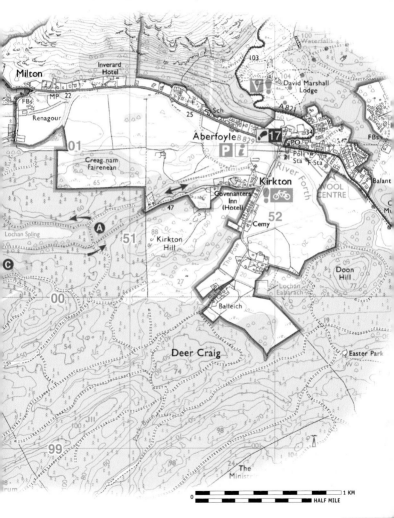

18 *Conic Hill*

START Balmaha
DISTANCE 6 miles (9.7km)
TIME 3–3½ hours
PARKING Balmaha
ROUTE FEATURES Roads, tracks, moorland paths, hill paths, steep descent

Boasting one of the finest views of Loch Lomond, Conic Hill is a rewarding ascent. Taken direct from Balmaha, it can be climbed in an hour, but this approach wanders off in completely the wrong direction before gradually looping back to share the climb with West Highland Wayfarers. Dogs are prohibited on Conic Hill, as is access during lambing time (April–May).

Leave the car park at Balmaha by turning left and walking along the roadside footpath (part of the West Highland Way) all the way to Milton of Buchanan, a distance of 1½ miles (2.5km).

Ⓐ Turn left at the postbox into Creityhall Road, and follow a rough track, ascending gently, into the fringe of the Garadhban Forest until it meets the West Highland Way at an obvious cross track.

Conic Hill from the West Highland Way near Drymen

Ⓑ At a WHW waymark, go left soon entering Garadh Ban Wood through which the path eases on before finally emerging at a broad stile across a deer fence with open moorland ahead.

PUBLIC TRANSPORT Buses to Balmaha
REFRESHMENTS Balmaha
PUBLIC TOILETS In visitor centre
ORDNANCE SURVEY MAPS Explorer 347 (Loch Lomond South), Landranger 56 (Loch Lomond & Inveraray)

Loch Lomond from Conic Hill

Leave the forest behind and follow a wide grassy path that initially sweeps out onto the moors before changing direction and heading directly for Conic Hill. Cross the tree-lined gorge of the Burn of Mar and climb a flight of steps which starts the ascent of Conic Hill itself.

C Above the steps, the path continues steadily upwards, nowhere difficult but best taken at a relaxed pace. Gradually, Loch Lomond eases into view, as does Ben Lomond, the Luss Hills and the cluster of high mountains around Ben Vorlich. There can be no better view of Loch Lomond than this, sweeping away majestically into the blue haze of hills above Glen Falloch.

D A large cairn marks the start of the descent to Balmaha. The summit of Conic Hill requires a diversion along a diagonal path slanting upwards from the highest point of the main path.

From the high point, go down steadily. The path is clear, *but conditions underfoot can be slippery when wet*. After the

> **Conic Hill** lies along the Highland Boundary Fault, a great geological crack that separates the rough Highland terrain to the north from the softer, sandstone lowlands. The fault, which can be seen continuing across Loch Lomond as a line of islands, runs for 160 miles (260km) from the island of Arran, in the Clyde, to Stonehaven on the east coast.

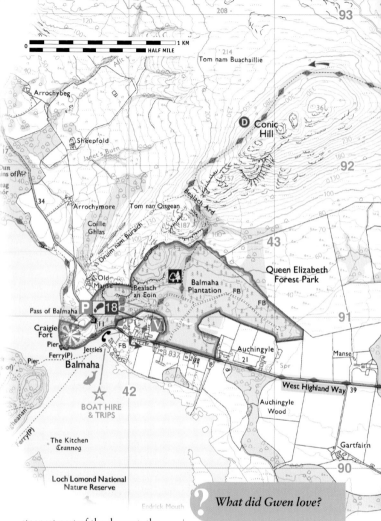

What did Gwen love?

steepest part of the descent, the path divides near the Bealach Ard. Here branch left, crossing the main thrust of the hill, and dropping into a small hollow before swinging round to face Loch Lomond again.

At the foot of the hollow a right turn leads across a terrace path above a ravine, beyond which a flight of steps eases the path downwards towards the boundary of the Balmaha Forest.

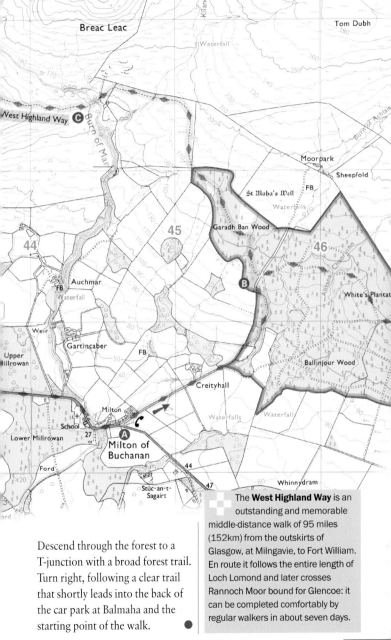

Descend through the forest to a T-junction with a broad forest trail. Turn right, following a clear trail that shortly leads into the back of the car park at Balmaha and the starting point of the walk. ●

The **West Highland Way** is an outstanding and memorable middle-distance walk of 95 miles (152km) from the outskirts of Glasgow, at Milngavie, to Fort William. En route it follows the entire length of Loch Lomond and later crosses Rannoch Moor bound for Glencoe: it can be completed comfortably by regular walkers in about seven days.

19 Garadhban Forest

START North of Drymen
DISTANCE 6 miles (9.5km)
TIME 2½–3 hours
PARKING Roadside
ROUTE FEATURES Woodland trails, lanes, field tracks, roads

Offering a taste of the West Highland Way (in the hope of encouraging walkers to attempt the whole thing), this easy walk begins with the stretch through the Garadhban Forest before heading down towards the Buchanan Estate. The views (once out of the forest) are consistently good and inspiring.

[Walkers using public transport can elect to begin either at Buchanan Smithy or Milton of Buchanan.]

Set off along the forest trail from the roadside bend until it intercepts another. Now turn right and walk up to a T-junction, where the West Highland Way is encountered. Turn left. The on-going track is clear throughout the forest, waymarked (white thistle on post) as necessary, and ignores all branching tracks and paths.

The track finally emerges from the forest at another metal barrier, and

Garadhban Forest is managed by Forest Enterprise and forms part of the much larger, but not entirely wooded, Queen Elizabeth Forest Park. In summer, the forest is alive with members of the tit family, and in autumn puts on a good display of mushrooms and toadstools. Although seeming impenetrable within a few strides of the trail, the forest is never dark and oppressive, and open enough in places to give occasional glimpses of far blue hills.

then goes forward to a track junction **A**. Turn left here, leaving the West Highland Way to contend with Conic Hill.

PUBLIC TRANSPORT Buses to Drymen, Buchanan Smithy and Milton of Buchanan
REFRESHMENTS Drymen
PUBLIC TOILETS Drymen
ORDNANCE SURVEY MAPS Explorer 347 (Loch Lomond South), Landranger 56 (Loch Lomond & Inveraray)

Garadhban Forest

A lovely track descends, with outstanding views north to Loch Lomond. During lambing time the West Highland Way is diverted along this stretch to avoid disturbance.

The descending track is flanked during summer by a diverse range of flowers – ragged robin, tormentil, buttercup, forget-me-not, red campion, dog rose – and provides a fine view northwards to Conic Hill.

The track eventually becomes Creityhall Road and eases down to meet the Balmaha road at Milton of Buchan. Turn left and follow the roadside footpath for about 400 yds (365m) as far as a bridge spanning a stream.

B Cross the road with care and go into a driveway opposite, immediately turning left along the Gort Daraich Walk, a broad semi-surfaced track flanked by mixed woodland.

The track passes a few isolated houses and then continues through open, mixed plantation of larch, spruce and pine.

When the on-going route reaches a T-junction, turn left, leaving the plantation for a track sandwiched between pastures. Press on through a neck of woodland before reaching another junction.

C Turn left and walk up to rejoin the Balmaha road opposite the Buchanan Smithy Cottages. Bear

Track junction near Coldrach Farm

right, crossing the road, and take the first turning on the left.

Go forward to walk up a rough track, later turning right to Coldrach Farm. Pass the farm and continue along the rough track beyond, with lovely elevated views of Strathendrick, until it meets a surfaced lane near Coldrach Lodge. Turn left and walk up the road to the start.

> **?** *Gorse is a common sight across many British heathlands, but on this walk broom, or furze, is equally dominant. Can you find some?*

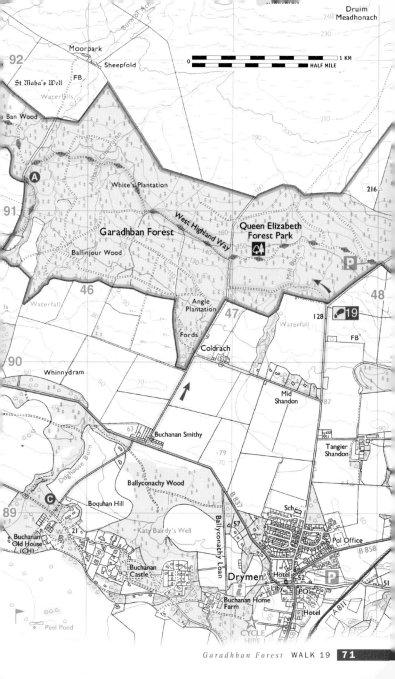

20 *Greenock Cut*

START Cornalees Bridge
DISTANCE 6¾ miles (11km)
TIME 2½–3 hours
PARKING Cornalees Bridge
ROUTE FEATURES Moorland tracks, upland paths

The circuit of Greenock Cut is largely about the man who built it, Robert Thom. But, although his legacy is a remarkable excuse for wandering the hills, the upland scenery – part of the Clyde Muirshiel Regional Park – speaks for itself: wild, rugged and extravagantly beautiful.

Leave the visitor centre at Cornalees Bridge and set off along the surfaced track, passing a compensation reservoir, to reach Loch Thom Cottage, where the dam of Loch Thom is reached.

Beyond the cottage, through a gate and just after a well built by the Argyll and Sutherland Highlanders, the track ceases to be surfaced and becomes stony as it climbs gently to a low pass Ⓐ between Jock's Hill and White Hill. There is a fine

The **Greenock Cut** was built by an outstanding water engineer, Robert Thom, who held the view that the hills above Greenock could be harnessed to produce substantial supplies of water to power the industries around the Clyde coast. The Cut, a man-made watercourse or leat, was the result, running from Loch Thom, also man-made, to Greenock – less than 2 miles (3.2km) by crow, but 6 miles (10km) by the Cut. Work was completed in 1827 at a cost of £52,000, and today this masterpiece of engineering is a scheduled ancient monument.

Can you find the dates 1827 and 1927?

retrospective view over Loch Thom to the Renfrewshire Hills.

PUBLIC TRANSPORT Buses along A78
REFRESHMENTS Visitor Centre
PUBLIC TOILETS At start
ORDNANCE SURVEY MAPS Explorer 341 (Greenock, Largs & Millport), Landranger 63 (Firth of Clyde)

Malevolent fishermen from Solomon Islands provide a surprise start to the walk

From this upland pass where Loch Thom finally passes from view, it's all downhill, passing two more reservoirs, to reach a whitewashed cottage on the edge of Overton **B**.

Cross a small bridge and immediately turn left alongside the Greenock Cut, which now contours across the hillside high above Greenock and Gourock.

Gradually, the Cut, having been pre-occupied with a plentiful series of twists and turns, changes direction **C** as it rounds Dunrod Hill, heading inland, finally to emerge onto a road at Shielhill Farm.

Greenock Cut

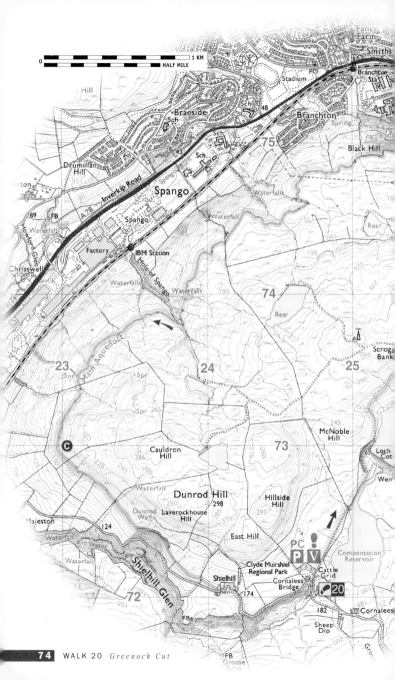

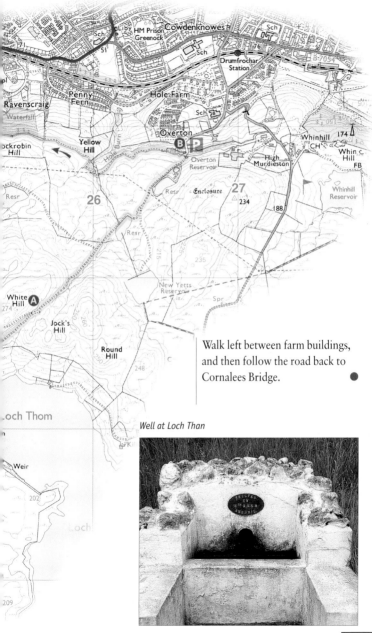

Walk left between farm buildings, and then follow the road back to Cornalees Bridge.

Well at Loch Than

Further Information

Walking Safety

Always take with you both warm and waterproof clothing and sufficient food and drink. Wear suitable footwear, i.e. strong walking boots or shoes that give a good grip over stony ground, on slippery slopes and in muddy conditions. Try to obtain a local weather forecast and bear it in mind before you start. Do not be afraid to abandon your proposed route and return to your starting point in the event of a sudden and unexpected deteriorationin the weather.

All the walks described in this book will be safe to do, given due care and respect, even during the winter. Indeed, a crisp, fine winter day often provides perfect walking conditions, with firm ground underfoot and a clarity of light unique to that time of the year.

The most difficult hazard likely to be encountered is mud, especially when walking along woodland and field paths, farm tracks and bridleways – the latter in particular can often get churned up by cyclists and horses. In summer, an additional difficulty may be narrow and overgrown paths, particularly along the edges of cultivated fields. Neither should constitute a major problem provided that the appropriate footwear is worn.

Follow the Country Code

- Enjoy the countryside and respect its life and work
- Guard against all risk of fire
- Take your litter home
- Fasten all gates
- Help to keep all water clean
- Keep your dogs under control
- Protect wildlife, plants and trees
- Keep to public paths across farmland
- Take special care on country roads
- Leave livestock, crops and machinery alone
- Make no unnecessary noise
- Use gates and stiles to cross fences, hedges and walls

(The Countryside Agency)

Useful Organisations

Forest Enterprise
231 Corstorphine Road, Edinburgh EH12 7AT. Tel: 01313 340303; Fax: 0131 334 3047.

Historic Scotland, Longmore House, Salisbury Place, Edinburgh EH9 1SH. Tel: 0131 668 8800

National Trust for Scotland,
Wemyss House, 28 Charlotte Square, Edinburgh EH2 4ET. Tel: 0131 243 9300; Fax: 0131 243 9301

Ordnance Survey
Romsey Road, Maybush, Southampton SO16 4GU. Tel: 02380 792912; Fax: (Public) 02380 792615; Website: www.ordsvy.gov.uk

Daffodils at Inchmahome Priory

Ramblers' Association
2nd Floor, Camelford House, 87–90 Albert Embankment, London SE1 7TW.
Tel: 020 7339 8585; Website: www.ramblers.org.uk.

Royal Society for the Protection of Birds (RSPB)
The Lodge, Sandy, Beds SG19 2DL. Tel: 01767 680551; Website: www.rspb.org.uk

Scottish Natural Heritage
Battleby, Redgorton, Perth PH1 3EW. Tel: 01738 627921

Scottish Wild Land Group
8 Hartington Place, Bruntsfield, Edinburgh EH10 4LE. Tel: 0131 229 2094.

Scottish Youth Hostels Association
7 Glebe Crescent, Stirling FK8 2JA. Tel: 01786 891400; Fax: 01786 891333; Website: www.syha.org.uk.

Local Organisations

Visit Scotland
23 Ravelston Terrace
Edinburgh EH4 3TP
Tel: 0131 332 2433
Fax: 0131 315 2906
Email: info@visitscotland.com
Website: www.visitscotland.net

Greater Glasgow & Clyde Valley Tourist Board
11 George Square
Glasgow G2 1DY
Tel: 0141 566 4056
Fax: 0141 204 4772

Argyll, the Isles, Loch Lomond, Stirling and the Trossachs Tourist Board
Old Town Jail

St John Street
Stirling FK8 1EA
Tel: 01786 445 222
Fax: 01786 471 301

Loch Lomond and The Trossachs National Park
The Old Station, Balloch G83 8SS.
Tel: 01389 722 600; Fax: 01389 722 633. Visitor Enquiries: Loch Lomond and The Trossachs National Park Gateway Centre. Tel: 01389 722 199

Local tourist information centres
Glasgow: 0141 204 4400
Aberfoyle: 08707 200 604
Abington: 01864 502 436
Balloch: 08707 200 607
Biggar : 01899 221 066

Callander: 08707 200 628
Drymen: 08707 200 611
Dumbarton: 08707 200 612
Dunblane: 08707 200 613
Glasgow Airport : 0141 848 4440
Hamilton : 01698 285 590
Lanark : 01555 661 661
Paisley: 0141 889 0711
Rothesay: 08707 200 619

Ordance Survey Maps
Explorer maps 335 (Lanark & Tinto Hills), 341 (Greenock, Largs & Millport), 342 (Glasgow), 343 (Motherwell & Coatbridge), 347 (Loch Lomond South), 348 (Campsie Fells), 362 (Cowal West & Isle of Bute) and 365 (The Trossachs). Landranger maps 56 (Loch Lomond & Inverarary), 57 (Stirling & The Trossachs), 63

Alongside Stathclyde Loch

(Firth of Clyde), 64 (Glasgow), and 72 (Upper Clyde Valley).

Answers to Questions

Walk 1: The lake is especially popular with swans, grey heron, coot, moorhen and great crested grebe.

Walk 2: The sculptures were designed by local artist, Robert Coia, to portray characteristic wildlife and the agricultural usage of the surrounding countryside.

Walk 3: 5th May 1883, aged 13 years. Near the end of the walk, at the side of the track, there is a small headstone for what was obviously a family pet.

Walk 4: Just after the metal bridge and before the jetty a small cliff on the left shows characteristic hallmarks of lava flowing over smooth, sea-washed rocks and pebbles. The layered rocks have later been tilted by earth movements.

Walk 5: The rocks just off the coast along this walk are popular basking places for common and grey seals. They tend to haul themselves onto the rocks towards the latter part of the day, but can often be found there early in the morning, too.

Walk 6: Small groups of grey wagtails (grey on top and yellow underneath) can usually be seen from White Bridge, flitting about the river or darting up to catch an air-borne insect.

Walk 7: The kestrels other name is the windhover from its apparent ability to hover stationary facing into the wind. It is the only bird that can do this, though buzzards sometimes give a passable impression.

Walk 8: Along the bridleway on the return leg of the walk, the upper woodland boundary is made up of coppiced beech, though it is more usual to see hazel used for this purpose. The pruned branches would be used for fencing, stockades and roofing.

Walk 9: Jungle. The word is painted onto a tree near the housing estate.

Walk 10: There are two stone lions either side of the river entrance to Pollok House.

Walk 11: The boats on the loch range from rescue vessels to pedalos, and include the rowing boats for one, two, four or eight people used by the academy as well as different shapes and sizes of small yacht.

Walk 12: This is the number on the trig pillar on Auchineden Hill.

Walk 13: Buzzards are usually heard before they are seen. They give a high-pitched mewing sound, rather like a kitten, and can often be spotted circling above fields and woodlands.

Walk 14: Although gannets tend to prefer more open water, they often patrol the Kyles of Bute and the Clyde, and are spectacular to watch.

Walk 15: On a clear day Skiddaw in the English Lake District can be seen 62½ miles (100km) to the south; Goat Fell on Arran lies 60 miles (95km) to the west, and Ben Cleuch in the Ochil Hills, 31 miles (50km) to the north.

Walk 16: There are plenty about, and on my last visit I saw four at very close range. A quiet approach is likely to bring its rewards.

Walk 17: As well as those mentioned in the text, you could reasonably expect to see grey herons around the lochan edges. A good field guide will help identify the different birds you will see.

Walk 18: The loch and the countryside. There is a memorial bench on the track continuation of Creityhall Road, with a lovely view of Loch Lomond.

Walk 19: Throughout most parts of the walk stands of broom feature alongside the route. With yellow flowers in summer, the thin, tough stems of the bush are a year-round presence.

Walk 20: These dates are those of the completion of the Greenock Cut and its centenary, and are found on a drinking fountain (obsolete) on the bridge beside the waterman's cottage at Overton.

JARROLD SHORT WALKS
leisure walks for all ages

Glasgow

Compiled by
Terry Marsh

JARROLD
publishing

Mapping
sourced from
Ordnance
Survey

Text: Terry Marsh
Photography: Terry Marsh
Editor: Crawford Gillan
Designer: Ellen Moorcraft

© Jarrold Publishing 2003

 Ordnance Survey® This product includes mapping data licensed from Ordnance Survey® with the permission of the Controller of Her Majesty's Stationery Office. © Crown Copyright 2002. All rights reserved. Licence number 100017593. Ordnance Survey, the OS symbol and Pathfinder are registered trademarks and Explorer, Landranger and Outdoor Leisure are trademarks of the Ordnance Survey, the national mapping agency of Great Britain.

Jarrold Publishing ISBN 0-7117-2426-1

First published 2003
by Jarrold Publishing

Printed in Belgium
by Proost NV, Turnhout. 1/03

Jarrold Publishing
Pathfinder Guides, Whitefriars,
Norwich NR3 1TR

E-mail: pathfinder@jarrold.com
www.jarrold-publishing.co.uk

Front cover: Along the track to Auchineden Hill
Previous page: In Bogany Wood